**M257** Unit 4
UNDERGRADUATE COMPUTING

# Putting Java to work

# Input, output and exceptions

Unit 4

This publication forms part of an Open University course M257 *Putting Java to work*. Details of this and other Open University courses can be obtained from the Student Registration and Enquiry Service, The Open University, PO Box 197, Milton Keynes MK7 6BJ, United Kingdom: tel. +44 (0)870 333 4340, email general-enquiries@open.ac.uk

Alternatively, you may visit the Open University website at http://www.open.ac.uk where you can learn more about the wide range of courses and packs offered at all levels by The Open University.

To purchase a selection of Open University course materials visit http://www.ouw.co.uk, or contact Open University Worldwide, Michael Young Building, Walton Hall, Milton Keynes MK7 6AA, United Kingdom for a brochure. tel. +44 (0)1908 858785; fax +44 (0)1908 858787; email ouwenq@open.ac.uk

The Open University
Walton Hall, Milton Keynes
MK7 6AA

First published 2007. Second edition 2008.

Edited, designed and typeset by The Open University.

Printed and bound in the United Kingdom by Hobbs the Printers Ltd.

ISBN 978 0 7492 6799 5

2.1

The paper used in this publication contains pulp sourced from forests independently certified to the Forest Stewardship Council (FSC) principles and criteria. Chain of custody certification allows the pulp from these forests to be tracked to the end use (see www.fsc-uk.org).

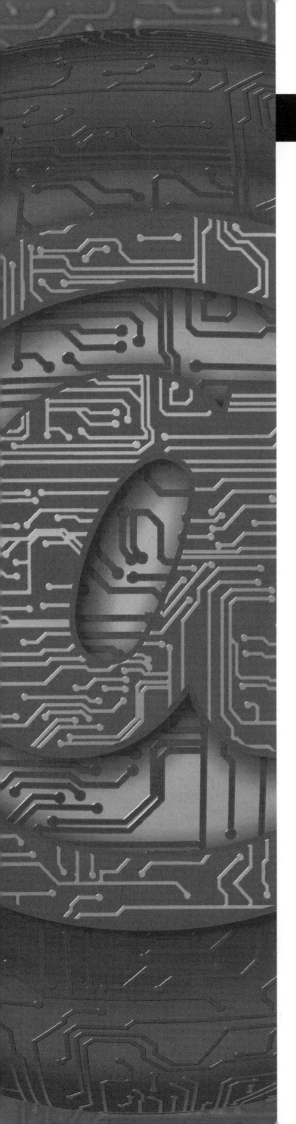

# CONTENTS

# M257 COURSE TEAM

M257 *Putting Java to work* was adapted from M254 *Java everywhere*.

M254 was produced by the following team.

**Martin Smith**, Course Team Chair and Author

**Anton Dil**, Author

**Brendan Quinn**, Author

**Janet Van der Linden**, Academic Editor

**Barbara Poniatowska**, Course Manager

**Ralph Greenwell**, Course Manager

**Alkis Stavrinides**, External Assessor, Coventry University

## Critical readers

**Pauline Curtis**, Associate Lecturer

**David Knowles**, Associate Lecturer

**Robin Walker**, Associate Lecturer

**Richard Walker**, Associate Lecturer

The M257 adaptation was produced by:

**Darrel Ince**, Course Team Chair and Author

**Richard Walker**, Consultant Author and Critical Reader

**Matthew Nelson**, Critical Reader

**Barbara Poniatowska**, Course Manager

**Ralph Greenwell**, Course Manager

**Alkis Stavrinides**, External Assessor, Coventry University

## Media development staff

**Andrew Seddon**, Media Project Manager

**Garry Hammond**, Editor

**Ian Blackham**, Editor

**Anna Edgley-Smith**, Editor

**Jenny Brown**, Freelance Editor

**Andrew Whitehead**, Designer and Graphic Artist

**Glen Derby**, Designer

**Phillip Howe**, Compositor

**Lisa Hale**, Compositor

Thanks are due to the Desktop Publishing Unit of the Faculty of Mathematics and Computing.

# 1 Introduction

Communication is vital. It is also potentially unreliable. This is true of human communication, but also of communication between humans and computers, or equally when one computer communicates with another across a network.

There are two fundamentally different ways of communicating with a Java program. In this unit we look at communicating with a sequential source or destination (such as a file, a keyboard or another computer). Later units deal with the alternative approach – constructing and using a graphical user interface. Java provides a rich and flexible set of facilities for sequential input and output, within a consistent framework. This makes the process of communication similar, whatever the source or destination of the data.

Many things can go wrong – the expected disk file may be missing or the network links may be faulty. So, in this unit, we also take the opportunity to consider how to deal with error conditions and unexpected events.

We discuss **exception handling**, the main approach in Java for dealing with serious or unpredictable error conditions. This can be applied to many different situations but is particularly relevant to communication and input/output since unexpected events may readily occur.

Finally, simple programming examples tend to ignore many possible complications, in the interests of simplicity of explanation. For example, when inserting items in a table we may assume that the table has enough room to contain each item. When we remove an item from a table, we may assume that the item is present in the table in the first place. A more robust approach cannot rely on these assumptions, and it is necessary to look at some of the techniques that can be used to cater for such predictable error conditions.

In this unit, we aim to:

▶ explain how Java handles input and output;

▶ demonstrate how input and output facilities deal with various types of data and a range of sources and destinations;

▶ show how to deal with error conditions in a Java program, by means of exceptions or otherwise;

▶ explain the various forms of Java exceptions, and how to write your own exception classes.

We begin by considering how to carry out input and output.

# 2 Input and output streams

Java relies on the concept of a **stream** for providing its input/output facilities. A stream, sometimes referred to as a **byte stream**, is essentially a sequence of bytes, representing a flow of data from a source to a destination. Java streams provide facilities to handle these flows of data in a consistent way for a wide variety of sources and destinations, including the keyboard, screen and various sorts of data files, as well as between networked computers. They also allow manipulation of the data on the way: for example, by converting the data to different formats or by storing it temporarily (buffering).

## 2.1 Streams everywhere

All the streams provided in Java can be found in the `java.io` package. Any program that uses streams needs to include the statement:

```
import java.io.*;
```

A glance at the online documentation for the `java.io` library shows a bewildering variety of different stream classes. Figures 1 to 4 show the class hierarchy for some of these.

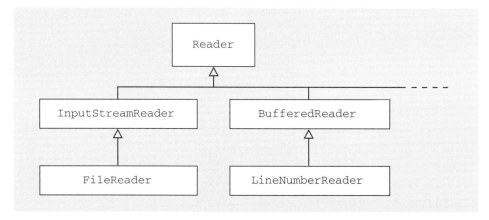

Figure 1    Partial class hierarchy of Java stream classes for character input

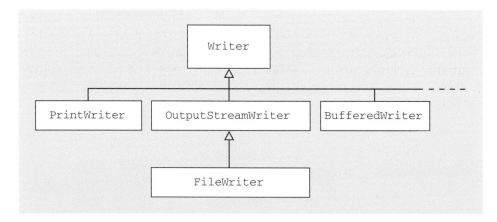

Figure 2    Partial class hierarchy of Java stream classes for character output

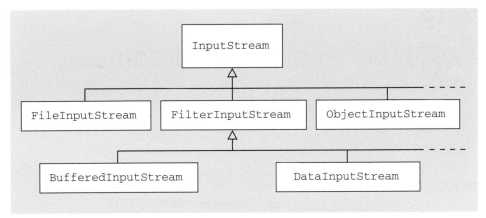

Figure 3    Partial class hierarchy of Java stream classes for byte input

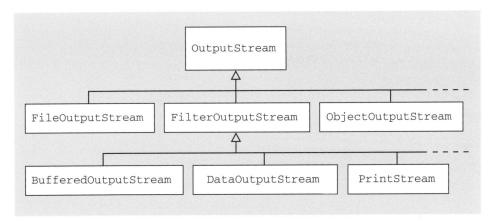

Figure 4    Partial class hierarchy of Java stream classes for byte output

We will explain the reason for the many different kinds and how to select the ones you need.

▶ There are streams for input, like `InputStreamReader`, and streams for output, like `OutputStreamWriter`.

▶ Some streams deal with data in terms of bytes, namely `InputStream`, `OutputStream` and their subclasses. Classes like `Reader`, `Writer` and their subclasses handle character data (recall that Java uses the two-byte Unicode representation of characters).

▶ We can also categorize streams into those that represent a source or a destination (such as a data file or a network connection), for example `FileReader`, as opposed to streams that allow modification or management of the stream data, such as `LineNumberReader` or `BufferedWriter`.

This wide variety can be confusing so in the following sections we shall look at some simple examples for typical input and output requirements. Note that the four classes that form the roots of the various hierarchies, namely `Reader`, `Writer`, `InputStream` and `OutputStream`, are all abstract classes. This means that you cannot create objects of these classes, only of their subclasses (we explain abstract classes in detail in the next unit). Fortunately, they have no shortage of subclasses, so this does not pose a problem.

## 2.2 Standard input and output streams

We have already encountered one stream object, namely `System.out` whose `println` method we have used to display information on the computer screen. For example:

```
System.out.println("The program has started");
```

The `System` class found in `java.lang` provides reference variables for three predefined streams, `System.in`, `System.out` and `System.err`. The standard input stream is `System.in` and it normally carries data from the keyboard of your computer; `System.out` is the standard output stream and is normally directed to a window on the screen of your computer; `System.err` can be used by the programmer to display error messages, and the destination is normally a screen window. All these three standard stream references are declared as `public` and `static`, so they can be conveniently accessed directly via the `System` class, without the need to create an object.

Recall that we cannot have objects of the abstract class `InputStream`.

The `System.out` and `System.err` streams are of type `PrintStream` and have `println` and `print` methods immediately available for use. The `System.in` stream is of the generic type `InputStream` and is not so straightforward to use. It must normally be used in combination with other streams.

## 2.3 Streams and exception handling

Input and output operations of all kinds are particularly likely to give rise to errors of the 'unexpected' kind, such as missing data files or errors in the format of input data. These situations are normally catered for in Java by means of exceptions. At the point in the code where the error occurs, we say the code throws an exception.

We shall see, later in this unit, the detail of how exceptions work and how to handle them. For the moment, we will deal with possible exceptions in a very simple way. Any method that could give rise to an input/output exception must declare this by adding `throws IOException` at the end of the method header, as in the following example:

```
public void openStreams (String fileName)
    throws IOException
{
    ...
}
```

Failure to declare this causes a compiler error. If such an exception does occur, the program will terminate with an error message indicating that an `IOException` has occurred.

# 3 Reading text input

In order to give you an idea of the power of using streams for input and output, we consider how to input text, first from the keyboard and then from a file. This shows how similar the programming of input is, regardless of the source. Normally we combine a source stream with one or more processing or data manipulation streams to get the desired behaviour. Java 1.5 introduces a convenience class for text processing called Scanner, in the java.util package.

## 3.1 Reading text from the keyboard

Recall that the keyboard is normally the source of data for the standard input stream System.in. This stream can be passed to an instance of Scanner to read keyboard input that may be returned as string or primitive data. An example is show below:

```
public void hello()
{
    Scanner sc = new Scanner(System.in);
    //Ask what is your name
    String name = sc.nextLine();
    //Ask what is your age
    int age = sc.nextInt();
    //Display name and age here
    sc.close();//take care
}
```

The program creates a Scanner object that reads data into an area of memory. It allows the user to enter a name and age and have the program repeat them back.

Note the use of the close method to close the Scanner when we have finished using it. This is usually good practice with streams and sometimes essential to proper operation, as a later example in this section will show. However, closing Scanner can also close its underlying stream, and so you should not normally close a Scanner unless you also opened its source. In this case, closing the Scanner closes System.in, which is probably to be avoided, as it will mean that you cannot read any further data from the keyboard.

## 3.2 Reading text from a file

**Activity 4.1**
Reading input from the keyboard.

To read text from a source other than the keyboard, we simply change the stream defining the source. So instead of using System.in, we can use a file. The Scanner class has a constructor receiving a File as an argument and then provides the same methods to read from the file. For example:

```
Scanner sc = new Scanner
    (new File ("source/use.txt"));
```

Note that the File constructor requires a string corresponding to the filename in a form appropriate to the local operating system. You can specify absolute or relative path names, such as:

```
"C:/javasource/datafiles/users.txt"
```

This uses the forward slash character as a separator and should work across all platforms. If you want to use Windows-style filenames, you must use a double backslash character to indicate the normal Windows filename separator (one backslash) like this:

```
"C:\\javasource\\datafiles\\users.txt"
```

This is because the backslash is used in strings to indicate escape characters, such as \n and \t for newline and tab respectively.

As usual, the close method of the Scanner class is invoked when we have finished reading the file. This ensures that any data still in a buffer is processed before the program continues.

**Activity 4.2**
Reading from a text file.

# Writing text output to a file

In previous versions of Java writing text to a file was a little complicated; the newest version of Java makes the whole process easier. The `PrintWriter` class provides methods for writing text and primitives to a named file. The constructor:

```
PrintWriter(String);
```

creates a file into which data can be written. For example, the code:

```
PrintWriter pw = new PrintWriter("Hello.txt");
```

will create a `PrintWriter` object that will write data to the text file `Hello.txt`. For example, the code:

```
pw.println("The first line");
pw.println("The second line");
```

will print two lines to the file. The only other operation that is needed with such a `PrintWriter` object is to close the file down by means of the `close` method so, for example, the code:

```
pw.close();
```

will close the file `Hello.txt` down.

The following class demonstrates the use of text output to a disk file. It generates a multiplication table and writes it to the file.

```java
import java.io.*;

public class MultiplicationTable
{
    PrintWriter out;

    final static int MAX_LINES = 10;

    public void openFile (String fileName) throws FileNotFoundException
    {
        out = new PrintWriter(fileName);
    }

    public void printMultiplicationTable ()
    {
        out.println("Multiplication Table");
        for (int i = 1; i <= MAX_LINES; i++)
        {
            out.print("line" + i + ":   ");
            for (int j = 1; j <= MAX_LINES; j++)
            {
                out.print("\t");
                out.print(i * j); //overloaded print()
            }
            out.println();
        }
    }
}
```

```
public void closeFile ()
{
    out.close ();
}
} // end class MultiplicationTable
```

The `MultiplicationTable` class can be used as follows:

```
import java.io.*;
public class TestMultiplicationTable
{
    public static void main (String [] args) throws FileNotFoundException
    {
        MultiplicationTable table = new MultiplicationTable ();
        table.openFile ("table.txt");
        table.printMultiplicationTable ();
        table.closeFile ();
    } // end main

} // end class TestMultiplicationTable
```

Note the use of the `closeFile` method, which invokes the `close` method of the `PrintWriter` class. This is known as **flushing** the buffer. This is essential to ensure that all the data is written to the file and does not remain unprocessed in the buffer – without this the file may be incomplete or even empty.

It can be done explicitly by invoking the flush method, for example, as follows:

```
out.print ("line" + i + ": ");
out.flush ();
```

It can also be done by using the `println` method.

The constructor for `PrintWriter (String)` within the method `openFile` will throw a `FileNotFoundException` if there is a problem either creating or accessing the file that is represented by the string argument.

The class `PrintWriter` is unusual among the stream classes in that its methods do not throw exceptions of type `IOException` when an error occurs. Instead, `PrintWriter` has a method called `checkError`, which returns a boolean value to indicate whether a problem has occurred when executing one of the methods of a given `PrintWriter` object. For example, using an extract from the previous example, we could check for an error like this:

```
out.print ("line" + i + ": ");
if (out.checkError ())
{
    System.err.println ("Faulty file output");
    out.close ();
    System.exit (-1);
}
```

**Activity 4.3**
Writing a date-stamp to a text file.

The call to `System.exit ()` will stop the program running. There is a convention to use a non-zero value to indicate abnormal termination.

# 5 Using data files

So far we have considered input from text files and output to text files. This sort of file can be read by people using a simple text editor or word processor.

It is also possible to write data to files so that it is stored in binary form: that is, essentially the same form in which it is stored in computer memory. The streams we have seen previously, like the various `Reader` and `Writer` streams, convert from this binary format in memory to text format for output – or from text to binary for input. Hence **binary input** and **binary output** are more efficient, since they avoid this conversion process. If the data files do not need to be human-readable this may be an appropriate format to use.

---

### Binary files

Java data files of this type are portable across platforms so, on some platforms, binary input/output may still require some conversion of internal binary formats to and from the portable binary format used by Java data files.

---

The stream classes that allow you to read and write data of primitive data types in binary form are `DataInputStream` and `DataOutputStream`. The `Scanner` class cannot process binary data correctly. You need to layer other streams on top of these basic streams to access convenient methods for reading data.

## 5.1 Reading data from files

Setting up data streams is similar to the process for text streams, shown earlier, except that they use the corresponding classes from the byte-oriented stream classes inheriting from `InputStream` and `OutputStream`. For example, to set up a `DataInputStream` for buffered binary input from a file, we have:

```
FileInputStream fis = new FileInputStream("payroll.dat");
DataInputStream dataIn = new DataInputStream(fis);
```

The `DataInputStream` classes have methods – such as `readInt`, `readFloat`, `readBoolean` – that return a value of the corresponding primitive data type.

For example, the following code would read an integer and a boolean value respectively from the `DataInputStream` object `dataIn` and store the values in appropriate variables:

```
int highValue = dataIn.readInt();
boolean moreItems = dataIn.readBoolean();
```

## 5.2 Writing data to files

Output of binary format data is done using the `DataOutputStream` class, which is the output analogue of the `DataInputStream` class. It allows writing data to a stream (typically to a file), which can be read back using a `DataInputStream` object.

The streams for this are set up as shown below. For example:

```
FileOutputStream fos = new FileOutputStream("payroll.dat");
DataOutputStream dataOut = new DataOutputStream(fos);
```

This creates a file called `payroll.dat` and prepares it for output of binary data, which is achieved by the use of `DataOutputStream` methods, such as `writeBoolean` and `writeLong`.

For example, if you wish to write a `boolean` value, `isFull`, and a long integer, `primeValue`, to a `DataOutputStream` referenced by `dataOut`, then this would be achieved by:

```
dataOut.writeBoolean(isFull);
dataOut.writeLong(primeValue);
```

## 5.3 Serialization: input and output of object data

The preceding sections have shown how to read and write items of primitive data types from files. A technique known as object serialization makes it possible to write complete objects to files, including any objects they may reference. These stored objects may later be read back from files, together with any objects they referred to, and used again in a program. This uses the `ObjectInputStream` and `ObjectOutputStream` classes and can be applied to any object that implements the `Serializable` interface (we shall discuss interfaces in the next unit). Serialization is also useful in communicating object data across network connections. Further details are outside the scope of this course, but interested readers may wish to follow up this useful facility in the Java documentation or in other literature.

### SAQ 1

What is the main difference between the `Reader` and `Writer` classes on the one hand and the `InputStream` and `OutputStream` classes on the other?

ANSWER.....................................................................................................................

The `Reader` and `Writer` classes and their subclasses are used for streams of data that consist of text in Unicode format. The `InputStream` and `OutputStream` classes and their subclasses are used for streams of data that consist of bytes.

Using appropriate constructors, it is possible to convert data flows between `Reader` and `Writer` format, which uses Unicode, and `InputStream` and `OutputStream` format. Either format can be used for text input and output but `Reader` and `Writer` classes are preferred because Unicode is more internationally portable.

# 6 Exceptions

We have seen that input and output may give rise to errors that generate Java exceptions. However, up to now we have not attempted to deal with these exceptions in any way other than terminating the program if something goes wrong.

In this section, we discuss exceptions in more detail and explain a more sophisticated approach to exception handling.

## 6.1 Exception handling

Java's exception handling can be used to deal with potentially serious or unpredictable error conditions, such as a missing data file. In its simplest form, it works like this:

1   When the Java system detects an error, it stops the normal flow of program execution.

2   A special kind of Java object, known as an **exception**, is created. This object holds some information about what has gone wrong. There are different kinds of exceptions for different sorts of error conditions.

3   Control is transferred from the part of your program where the error occurred to an **exception handler**, which deals with the situation.

4   The exception object is available to the exception handler code and can be used to help decide on the appropriate action. The appropriate action may be to attempt to recover from the error condition and continue execution, or it may be best to terminate execution of some or all of the program with a suitable error message.

There are some special terms used in describing exceptions. At the point in the code where the error occurs, we say the code **throws** an exception. The exception handler **catches** the exception. In some circumstances, a method must **declare** an exception: that is, it must state in the method header that it can potentially throw a particular type of exception. The detailed Java syntax for all these activities is given in the next section.

Typical examples of serious errors that could occur within a Java program are as follows:

▶   a program tries to read past the end of a data file;

▶   a program cannot find a specified input file;

▶   a program tries to connect to a website using an invalid address;

▶   a program runs out of memory;

▶   a method tries to access an array element whose index is larger than the upper limit of the array;

▶   an overflow condition occurs when the result of some arithmetic operation exceeds the limit for the primitive data types involved;

▶   a program expecting to read a file of integers finds a string value in the file;

▶   a method expecting an object reference encounters a null reference instead.

Appropriate use of exceptions can overcome some of the problems associated with such situations.

**Activity 4.4**
A program that throws an exception.

# 6.2 Checked and unchecked exceptions

We have seen that an exception in Java is an object and that there can be different types of exceptions for different situations. Figure 5 shows part of the hierarchy of Java exception classes.

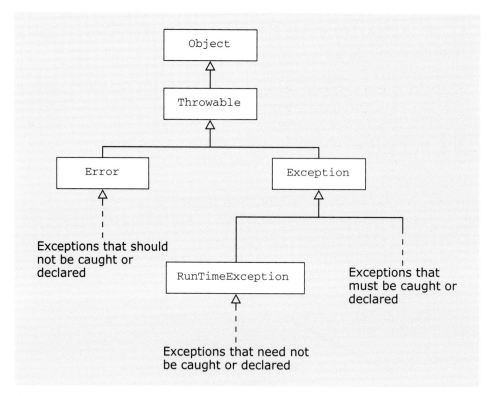

Figure 5    Part of the exception class hierarchy

The root of the exception inheritance tree is the class `Throwable`. This represents the most general class for describing exceptions.

The subclasses of `Throwable` can be divided into three main groups:

▶ the `Error` class and its subclasses;

▶ the `Exception` class and its subclasses, excluding the `RunTimeException` class and its subclasses;

▶ the `RunTimeException` class and its subclasses.

The error conditions corresponding to each of these three groups normally have different underlying causes and are treated differently by the Java system.

The class `Error` describes exceptions that occur when some internal Java error has happened – for example, the Java system has run out of memory. Such errors are rare and there is little that a programmer can do about them. The Java system monitors them and terminates the program, displaying some indication of what has happened.

Errors that are described by the class `Exception` and its subclasses can be monitored and acted on. Some of these are defined as **checked exceptions**. As you will see later in this unit, programmers must include code to declare or handle any checked exceptions that might occur. The Java compiler will report an error if this has not happened.

Checked exceptions include all exceptions of type `Exception` and of any subclasses of `Exception`, other than `RunTimeException` and its subclasses. Exceptions not covered by this definition are known, unsurprisingly, as **unchecked exceptions**.

## SAQ 2

Which classes in Figure 5 relate to unchecked exceptions and what does this mean for the programmer?

ANSWER........................................................................................................

From the definition above objects of type `Error` and any of its subclasses, and objects of type `RunTimeException` and any of its subclasses, are unchecked. This means that programmers do not need to include code to declare explicitly or handle exceptions of these types.

Java contains facilities for catching the exceptions that can occur during the running of a program. However, it is normally worth catching only exceptions relating to checked exception types. As we have seen, system errors described by the `Error` class are almost invariably fatal. Exceptions of type `RunTimeException` or its subclasses are normally due to programming errors – these should be eradicated by proper design, good programming style and exhaustive testing.

There are many built-in exception classes provided by the Java class library. These cover the most important errors that normally can occur within a Java program, but you can also define your own exception classes, as we show in a later section.

The following are examples of checked exceptions.

▶   `EOFException` occurs when a program attempts to read past the end of a file.

▶   `FileNotFoundException` can occur when a program attempts to open or write to an existing file. If the file cannot be found, then this exception is thrown.

▶   `MalformedURLException` indicates that an invalid form of URL (such as a website address) has occurred.

These are checked exceptions because they are subclasses of `IOException`, which is a direct subclass of `Exception` (see Figure 6).

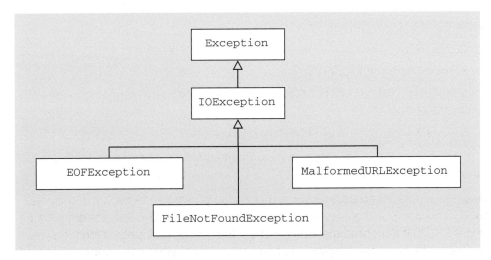

Figure 6   Inheritance hierarchy for some checked exceptions

The following are examples of unchecked exceptions, as they are subclasses of `RunTimeException`.

▶ `ArrayIndexOutOfBoundsException` occurs when a program tries to access an array with an index outside the valid limits.

▶ `ArithmeticException` arises when an illegal arithmetic condition occurs, such as an attempt to divide an integer by zero.

▶ `NumberFormatException` can be caused by an application expecting to read a number of some sort, when the data does not have the appropriate format.

▶ `NullPointerException` happens when an application attempts to use `null` in a case where an object is required: for example, invoking a method on a `null` reference.

# 7 Declaring and handling exceptions

If the code within a method may throw a checked exception, then you must do one of two things:

▶ declare in the method header that an exception may be thrown – in this case you do not handle the exception within the method, but simply pass it on;

▶ catch the exception and deal with it within the method, using a `try-catch` statement.

In this section we look at these two options.

## 7.1 Declaring exceptions

When declaring an exception in the method header, you use the keyword `throws` followed by the type of exception expected. We have seen this earlier in Section 4. A further example is shown below, for a method that might be used to check that a particular data file had the expected format:

```
public boolean checkFormat (String fileName)
    throws EOFException
{
    // code for method checkFormat
}
```

If the method unexpectedly came to the end of the file when expecting to read more data, then the method would generate an exception of type `EOFException`.

The keyword `throws` advertises that the method is capable of throwing an exception. In any code that uses this method some action will need to be taken to cater for this exception.

A method may be capable of generating more than one type of checked exception. In this case you need to list all the possible types, for example like this:

```
public boolean checkFormat (String fileName)
    throws EOFException, MalformedURLException
{
    // code for method checkFormat
}
```

If some or all of the possible exception types in a list are subclasses of a particular exception class, it may be possible to shorten the list. For example, instead of the above, we could write:

```
public boolean checkFormat (String fileName)
    throws IOException
{
    // code for method checkFormat
}
```

This works because `EOFException` and `MalformedURLException` are subclasses of `IOException`.

## 7.2 | Handling exceptions

We now know how to indicate that a method throws one or more exceptions. To deal with an exception that has been thrown, we use a `try-catch` statement. The simplest case is when only one type of exception is expected. For example, if `checkFormat` is invoked by another method, `loadFiles`, in the same class:

```
public void loadFiles ()
{
    ...
    try
    {
        if (checkFormat("File1.dat"))
        {
            // code to process file data
        }
    }
    catch (EOFException eofEx)
    {
        // code to handle this exception
        // eofEx refers to EOFException object
    }
}
```

The `try-catch` statement is made up of two parts – the `try` block and the `catch` clause. The `try` block contains the code that may throw an exception. If the exception occurs, the code within the `catch` clause will be executed; the `catch` clause handles the exception.

### SAQ 3

The `loadFiles` method used the `try-catch` option to deal with the possibility of exceptions. Which other option could the `loadFiles` method use?

ANSWER....................................................................................................................

It could declare the exception in the method header:

```
public void loadFiles () throws EOFException
```

Hence, if such an exception did occur, it would be passed up to the method that invoked `loadFiles`.

If more than one type of exception is possible, we can add additional `catch` clauses, like this:

```
try
{
    if (checkFormat("File1.dat"))
    {
        // code to process file data
    }
}
catch (EOFException eofEx)
{
    // code to handle end of file exception
    // eofEx refers to an EOFException object
}
catch (MalformedURLException urlEx)
{
    // code to handle bad URL exception
    // urlEx refers to a MalformedURLException object
}
...
```

The code in the `try` block is executed; if an exception is thrown the `try` block is exited and the appropriate exception handler code, if any, is executed. The exception handling code that is executed depends on which exception has been thrown.

The system checks each `catch` clause in turn for one that matches the type of the exception object. If the exception was an object described by the class `EOFException`, then the code immediately following:

```
catch (EOFException eofEx)
{
```

is executed, and so on. A more subtle point is that this handler will be selected if the exception object is either of type `EOFException` or of any subclass of `EOFException`.

When this handler code is executed, the variable within the `catch` clause will contain a reference to the exception object that has been thrown. For example, in the handler for `EOFException` the variable `eofEx` will contain a reference to the exception object.

If the code throws an exception that is not handled in any `try–catch` statement within the method, then the exception will be passed to the method that invoked this method. Any exception not handled in a particular method will be passed up a chain of invoking methods to a higher level, until an appropriate exception handler is found. This is known as **propagating** the exception, as shown in Figure 7. If no handler exists at any level for this exception, then the program terminates with an error message.

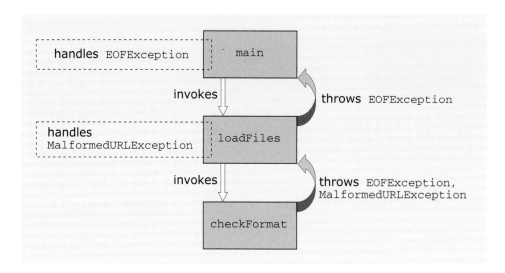

Figure 7    Example of propagating and handling exceptions

Recall that if the code within a method may throw a checked exception then you must do one of two things:

►   advertise in the method header that an exception may be thrown, and pass it on to the next level to deal with;

►   catch the exception within the method.

The Java compiler enforces these rules. If the first option is adopted you are assuming that the exception will be propagated to some other method, which will have the same options – to catch and handle the exception or to pass it on. A given method may have both a `throws` declaration in the header and a `try-catch` statement within the method – normally these would be for different types of exception.

## SAQ 4

What would happen if we extended the `try-catch` statement in the `loadFiles` method to deal with general I/O exceptions as well as the more specific ones in the original? This is shown in the code below:

```
try

{

    if (checkFormat("File1.dat"))

    {

        // code to process file data

    }

}

catch (IOException ioEx)

{

    // code to handle any I/O exception

    // ioEx refers to an IOException object

}
```

```
catch (EOFException eofEx)

{

    // code to handle end of file exception

    // eofEx refers to an EOFException object

}

catch (MalformedURLException urlEx)

{

    // code to handle bad URL exception

    // urlEx refers to a MalformedURLException object

}
```

ANSWER............................................................................................................

The first catch clause would handle all the exceptions including the more specific ones, as they are both subclasses of IOException. The compiler would detect this and flag an error to indicate that the second and third catch clauses would never be used. For this to work properly, we would need to change the order so that the catch clause for IOException came last, after the more specific exception clauses.

## What the exception handler can do

You may be wondering what an exception handler can do in response to any of the various potentially serious errors we have described. There are several possibilities: it can convey detailed information about the source of the problem; it may be able to 'tidy up' and release various resources in use by the program so that other parts of the system can carry on using them; in some cases, it may be able to allow further attempts to run the failing code – for example, to overcome temporary communication faults or incorrectly entered information.

The first option – reporting the source of the problem in detail – is probably the most important use of exceptions, and we consider this now. As you will see in the next section, an exception can have an associated message giving some additional information about the circumstances that gave rise to the error. If the code that caught an exception wants to examine this string it can use the method available to all exception objects, called getMessage.

For example:

```
try
{
    // code that may throw an Exception
}
catch (Exception ex)
{
    String errMessage = ex.getMessage();
    System.out.println("Error:" + errMessage);
    // rest of handler code
}
```

This code assigns to the string errMessage the message string associated with the exception, ex, and then displays an error message.

## SAQ 5

What happens if a method may throw an exception, but it neither catches the exception nor declares it in the method header?

ANSWER...................................................................................................................

The answer depends on whether the exception is a checked or an unchecked exception.

If it is a checked exception then this situation will give rise to a compiler error, and so the program could not be run.

For an unchecked exception, this situation is perfectly legal. This exception will be propagated: that is, passed on to the method that invoked the first method, and passed on further until an appropriate exception handler is found. If there is no such handler, the program will terminate with an error message.

### What the exception handler should not do

It is very important that an exception handler does not just 'bury' the exception by catching it and then taking no action, like this:

```
try
{
    // code that raises an IOException
}
catch (IOException ex) {}
```

There can be a temptation for programmers to do this as a quick way of suppressing a compiler error due to not handling a checked exception. This is very poor practice – it can temporarily conceal faults in a program, which may have more serious consequences at a later stage. If a particular method cannot do anything specific to handle an exception then it is normally best to pass it on, by declaring it in the method header, rather than 'burying' it. In the rare cases where there may be special reasons for having an empty exception handler, these should be clearly documented by program comments.

## 7.3 Cleaning up: the `finally` clause

One of the things we often want to do after an exception has occurred is to 'clean up' by releasing any resources such as memory or files that a method has been using before the exception was thrown. This allows these resources to be used by other parts of the program or other programs.

We can do this in a `catch` clause, but if we have several `catch` clauses this may require repeating the clean-up code in each `catch` clause, as well as within the `try` block to deal with normal execution. In this situation, it is easy to omit accidentally the clean-up code from one of the `catch` clauses – such errors are often hard to find.

To deal with this, Java provides another facility in the `try` statement – the `finally` clause. Code in the `finally` clause will be executed at the end of the `try` statement, whether or not execution was interrupted by an exception. If an exception occurred then the appropriate `catch` clause, if any, will be executed, followed by the code in the `finally` clause. If an exception did not occur, all the code in the `try` block would be executed followed by the clean-up code in the `finally` clause.

# 8 Throwing exceptions and creating your own

We have described how to deal with exceptions that may be generated by library classes, or by other people's code. But how are these exceptions generated? When we detect a problem, how do we create an exception object? In this section, we study how to create exceptions from the Java class library and how to define our own classes of exceptions.

## 8.1 Throwing exceptions

When we detect a problem, we can create an exception object by using the keyword `throw`. By way of example, we look in a little more detail at the `checkFormat` method introduced earlier. Suppose we expect the file we are checking to be structured into a header section of a certain fixed length (defined by the constant value `HEADER_LENGTH`), followed by various other sections. If we unexpectedly come to the end of the file before the number of characters expected in the header has been read, we can throw an exception. In this case, an appropriate choice would be an exception of the class `EOFException`.

```
public boolean checkFormat (String fileName)
    throws EOFException
{
    // part of code for method checkFormat
    ...
    int charsInHeader;
    charsInHeader = readHeader(file, header);
    if (charsInHeader < HEADER_LENGTH)
    {
        throw new EOFException();
    }
    ...
}
```

Note the use of the `new` operator and empty brackets after `EOFException` in the `throw` statement. This indicates that we are using a constructor for the `EOFException` class: in particular, the constructor that has no arguments.

Exceptions within the Java class library can be created using a zero-argument constructor, like this, or using a one-argument constructor. The one-argument constructor allows us to add a string to indicate some more detail about what has happened to cause the exception. In the example above, if we wanted to pass more information back to the code that calls the `checkFormat` method, we could write the `throw` statement like this:

```
throw new EOFException
    ("EOF error at file position " + charsInHeader);
```

This associates a string with the exception object, giving more details about the circumstances of the error. In this case, the string consists of some informative text together with the value of the variable `charsInHeader`, which indicates how far through the file the error occurred. This string is the one that can be accessed in the exception handler, using the `getMessage` method discussed earlier.

**Activity 4.5**
Developing a class that throws exceptions.

## 8.2 Creating your own exception classes

Even though the Java class library defines a large number of exceptions, there may be times when you want to define your own exceptions that correspond to error conditions that are specific to a particular application. Since exceptions are just objects, all you need do is create a new class that inherits from one of the exception classes that are provided as part of the Java class library (normally Exception or a checkable subclass of Exception).

For example, if we wanted to have a more specific exception type for the file format error above, we could define a new exception type like this:

```java
class FileFormatException extends IOException
{
    private int errorPosition;

    public FileFormatException () {}

    public FileFormatException (String message,
                                    int bytesRead)
    {
        super(message);
        errorPosition = bytesRead;
    }

    public int getErrorPosition ()
    {
        return errorPosition;
    }
}
```

Most exception classes have two constructors – a constructor with no arguments, and a one-argument constructor that allows for a more detailed error message. In this case, we have a constructor with no arguments and one with two arguments. This makes it possible to store and retrieve more detailed information on the location of the error within the file.

This exception can then be used within code in the same way that standard Java exceptions can be used. For example, in a method header:

```java
public boolean checkFormat (String fileName)
    throws FileFormatException
```

Our new exception can also be used in a try–catch statement:

```java
try
{
    // code to be checked
    if (checkFormat(theNewFile))
    {
        ...
    }
}
catch (FileFormatException exception)
{
    String reason = exception.getMessage();
    int errLoc = exception.getErrorPosition();
    System.out.println(reason+" at "+errLoc);
}
```

**Activity 4.6**
Writing a user-defined exception class.

---

### A very costly exception

On 4 June 1996, the maiden flight of the European Space Agency rocket launcher Ariane 5 ended in a spectacular failure. About 40 seconds after take-off, at an altitude of about 3700 m, Ariane 5 veered off its flight path, broke up and exploded. The launcher was carrying four expensive scientific satellites, all of which ended up as debris scattered over the swamps of French Guiana. It had taken the European Space Agency (ESA) 10 years and 7 billion dollars to develop Ariane 5.

After detailed investigations by ESA the cause of the crash was identified as a fault in the software controlling the inertial reference system that tracks the angle and velocity of the rocket. The software tried to convert a data item – the 'horizontal bias' of the rocket – from a 64-bit floating point format to a 16-bit integer format. The number was too big and an overflow exception resulted.

This exception was not caught by an exception handler. ESA had wrongly calculated that such an overflow could not occur and so no exception handler was needed. Hence it caused the inertial reference computer system to shut down – the duplicate system provided for back-up shut down for the same reason, as it had the same software. Ariane's main computers then had incorrect information about the position and direction of the rocket and proceeded to try to correct its direction, even though it was essentially on course. When the rocket tilted so much that it was in danger of breaking up, it was automatically destroyed by its on-board safety systems, making one of the world's most expensive firework displays! Fortunately, no-one was hurt. A full report with more technical details is available from ESA.

---

## 8.3 How to use exception handling

We have seen how to use a `try-catch` statement to identify program code that may cause an exception and how to deal with particular exceptions that may arise. There are some additional issues about how best to use this facility.

Firstly, it is best to be as specific as possible about the type of exception you expect to be generated. For example, it is usually a bad idea to do this:

```
try
{
    // code that may throw various exceptions
}
catch (Exception ex)
{
    // code that handles any exception
}
```

Using specific types of exception in the `catch` clauses has advantages. It documents the types of exception expected and also allows the exception handlers to deal more specifically with each type of exception.

Secondly, you do not have to deal with every possible type of exception. Any exception that cannot usefully be dealt with inside a particular method can be passed on to a higher level. This is another reason to be specific about the types of exception in the `catch` clauses.

It is possible and sometimes helpful to have more than one `try` statement within a method. This clearly defines the area of code where each exception is expected to arise:

```
try
{
    // code that may throw a FileNotFoundException
}
catch (FileNotFoundException ex)
{
    // code that handles a FileNotFoundException
}
//
// other code
//
try
{
    // code that may throw an EOFException
}
catch (EOFException ex)
{
    // code that handles an EOFException
}
```

There is clearly a balance to be struck here. Having one, possibly rather large `try` block may make it hard to identify which type of exception occurs where. It may also encourage the undesirable 'one size fits all' style of exception handling that we saw at the start of this subsection. On the other hand, having too many separate `try` blocks may clutter up the rest of the code and make it less readable. The choice is a matter of professional judgement.

# 9 Other error-handling techniques

Exceptions are not the only way to deal with problems and errors that may occur when a program runs. In this section we consider some standard programming techniques for handling error conditions and discuss when it is appropriate to use them.

## 9.1 Defensive programming

There are techniques to deal with potential errors, which are based on anticipating the conditions under which errors will occur. The first technique is to have a method return a value indicating whether the error condition was met when performing the code within the method.

For example, assume that we are writing a method called `add`, which adds an item to some data structure such as a queue of a fixed maximum size. You can imagine such a queue as being implemented by an array or some similar structure. Being a queue, it will have specific rules as to where elements can be added (only at the 'back' of the queue) and how elements can be taken out of the queue (only from the 'front' of the queue, not from the middle or the back). Normally the `add` method would return no value and would just add the element to the end of the queue. If the queue is already full, an error will occur. In order to cater for this error condition a `boolean` return value could be used. For example, the definition of such a method for a queue of strings might be:

```
public boolean add (String newItem)
{
    if (isFull()) // private helper method isFull
    {
        return false; // queue full, item not added
    }
    else
    {
        // code to add item to end of queue
        // ...
        return true; // item added successfully
    }
}
```

If the queue is full, then the method immediately returns the boolean value `false` and the new item is not added.

This approach has limitations – some methods may already return a result and it may not be possible to return an error indication as well.

The second technique – really a variation on the first approach – is to use a special method to check for a potential error condition *before* executing code that may encounter the condition. As above, assume that we are writing a public method called `add` that adds an item to a queue of fixed size. Before executing this method it would be wise to invoke another public method called, say, `isFull`, which would check that the queue had space for the item to be added. If it did not, then the method `add` would

**Activity 4.7**
Defensive programming.

not be invoked and the program would have to take some alternative action. This might be used as follows, where `q` is a suitably defined object of a queue class:

```
if (q.isFull())
{
    // carry out alternative action
}
else
{ // queue has space – so add new item
    q.add(newItem);
}
```

This second approach is related to an idea called **design by contract**. Here we are using the word 'contract' in the business sense to mean a well-defined agreement between two or more participants. The `add` method guarantees to add the item if there is space in the queue, as indicated by the `isFull` method. If there is no space in the queue then the 'contract' condition does not hold and the result of trying to add an item is not guaranteed (and will usually cause a problem, often throwing some sort of `RunTimeException`).

Both of the above approaches to error conditions are part of what is sometimes called **defensive programming**. This involves anticipating possible errors and including code to prevent them or to take appropriate action if errors do occur.

**Activity 4.8**
Designing by contract.

## 9.2 Defensive programming compared to exception handling

When should you use exceptions and when should you use defensive programming?

The defensive programming style of coding is appropriate for certain kinds of common error conditions. However, it has some drawbacks:

▶ if there is a lot of error checking and handling code, this can obscure the main purpose of the method;

▶ it is somewhat ad-hoc – different programmers or Java library code may take different approaches to signalling or handling errors;

▶ some serious errors cannot easily be handled within the method where they occur – they may need to be passed to higher level code;

▶ it may not be possible for a method to return a value indicating that an error has occurred – for example, if the method already returns a result.

Exception handling is intended for conditions that are:

▶ serious – they may require the program to be terminated;

▶ unpredictable – they may be caused by external events out of the control of the program, such as file errors;

▶ widespread – they may occur at many different places in the program, making it hard to check explicitly.

Often, you have no choice – for example, when dealing with potential exceptions generated by Java library classes.

Defensive programming techniques are appropriate when the potential error is more localized and predictable – for example, checking that a queue is not full before attempting to add a new element.

Exception handling is typically much slower in execution than standard error-handling techniques – this is a reason to use it sparingly.

There are 'grey areas' about when it is best to use exceptions and even the Java libraries sometimes may not seem to have a fully consistent approach. However, you should realize that if you omit the sort of defensive programming described above, this may well give rise to exceptions of type `RunTimeException`. This is usually an indication that your code is not robust enough.

# 10 The `StringTokenizer` class

Particularly when processing input data, there is often a need to read a string and split it up into individual **tokens**, each one representing a separate, meaningful item, such as a number or a word. In many programming languages such a process is complex to program, but the `java.util` library class `StringTokenizer` makes this very easy. An example of a `StringTokenizer` object is shown below:

```
StringTokenizer tokensIn =
    new StringTokenizer(stringIn," \n\t\r");
```

This sets up a tokenizer that allows extraction from the string `stringIn` of all the substrings that are terminated by any of the **delimiter** characters. The delimiter characters are within the string that is the second argument of the constructor – in this case, space, newline, tab and carriage return. These characters are collectively known as **white space**. Thus it picks up any substring that is terminated by white space and, of course, the final substring.

The `StringTokenizer` class includes two important methods, which carry out traversal of the string and checking that the final substring has been extracted.

▶ `String nextToken()` extracts the next string delimited by any of the delimiter characters and prepares the tokenizer for extraction of the following token. If there are no tokens left when this method is called, a `NoSuchElementException` will be thrown (but see `hasMoreTokens()`).

▶ `boolean hasMoreTokens()` returns `true` if there are more tokens to be processed in the string that is being traversed.

An example of this class being used is shown below. It shows code that finds, within the string `eMailAddress`, the component substrings that are terminated by a full stop, the @ symbol or the end of the string. It then prints these out.

```
StringTokenizer em = new StringTokenizer(eMailAddress, "@.");
while (em.hasMoreTokens())
{
    System.out.println(em.nextToken());
}
```

Since Java 5, a new approach to breaking strings into tokens is to use the `String.split()` method, which requires you to understand what are known as 'regular expressions'.

The `StringTokenizer` class is now considered a legacy class and is therefore no longer the recommended way to split strings, but has been retained because you are likely to encounter it in recent code and because you can use it without studying regular expressions.

## SAQ 6

State what printed output you would expect from the above fragment of `StringTokenizer` code if `eMailAddress` refers to the following text string:

> `"T.F.Jones@coolmail.com  Tom Jones"`

ANSWER..................................................................................................

In this case, only the delimiters '@' and '.' are used, so the string will be broken up into substrings bounded by these characters and the start and end of the whole string. Any embedded spaces will be ignored, since the space character was not included in the string of delimiter characters. The output will be:

```
T
F
Jones
coolmail
com  Tom Jones
```

**Activity 4.9**
Processing a CSV file.

# 11 Summary

This unit has described a number of ways in which Java programs can process sequential data input and output. The essential concept was the stream – an object that is used to read data from and write data to files and input/output devices.

Exceptions are a very powerful means of detecting and acting on unexpected or unpredictable events. Exceptions are objects; they are generated using the `throw` facility and are monitored using `try-catch` statements. Exceptions are classified as checked, which programs must check for and handle, and unchecked, which usually just cause program termination. If the code in a method throws a checked exception then the exception may be caught within the method, using a `try-catch` statement. Otherwise, the header for the method *must* advertise the fact that the method throws the exception, by using the keyword `throws`.

However, exceptions are not appropriate in all cases. More direct checks for predictable error conditions should be used, where appropriate, to ensure programs are robust and, as far as possible, do not generate run-time errors. This is known as defensive programming.

Finally we looked at a useful facility for extracting substrings from a string, the `StringTokenizer` class. This is particularly useful in processing complex data that was input in string form.

## LEARNING OUTCOMES

When you have completed this unit, you should be able to:

▶ explain the concept of a stream;

▶ use the basic Java facilities for input and output;

▶ input data from and output data to sequential files;

▶ distinguish text input/output from binary input/output;

▶ identify when it is appropriate to use exceptions;

▶ distinguish between checked and unchecked exceptions;

▶ define and use new types of exception;

▶ deal with error conditions in a Java program, by means of exceptions or otherwise;

▶ use the `StringTokenizer` class to split string data into substrings.

## Concepts

The following concepts have been introduced in this unit:

binary input/output, buffered input/output, checked exception, defensive programming, delimiter, design by contract, exception, exception handler, exception handling, exception propagation, flushing, stream, `StringTokenizer` class, text input/output, `throw`, token, `try-catch` statement, unchecked exception, white space.

# Index